THE PIECES OF MY LIFE

What it takes good and bad to make us
who we are in the scheme of things

Puzzling Indeed!

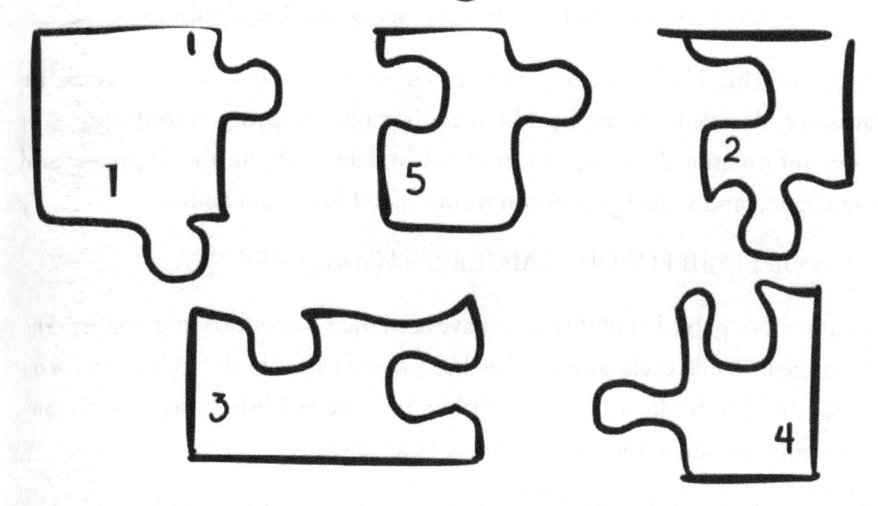

BY NANCY E. DIAMOND

© 2024 ALL RIGHTS RESERVED.

Published by She Rises Studios Publishing www.SheRisesStudios.com.

No part of this book may be reproduced or transmitted in any form whatsoever, electronic, or mechanical, including photocopying, recording, or by any informational storage or retrieval system without the expressed written, dated and signed permission from the publisher and author.

LIMITS OF LIABILITY/DISCLAIMER OF WARRANTY:

The author and publisher of this book have used their best efforts in preparing this material. While every attempt has been made to verify the information provided in this book, neither the author nor the publisher assumes any responsibility for any errors, omissions, or inaccuracies.

The author and publisher make no representation or warranties with respect to the accuracy, applicability, or completeness of the contents of this book. They disclaim any warranties (expressed or implied), merchantability, or for any purpose. The author and publisher shall in no event be held liable for any loss or other damages, including but not limited to special, incidental, consequential, or other damages.

ISBN: 978-1-960136-72-5

DEDICATION

This book is dedicated to my wonderful husband and to my daughters. Though they may be stepdaughters, they are truly the children of my heart. I could not love them more if they had been born to me. I relish the fact that they are all very different. They are all strong, successful women whom I admire. When I told my mother I would marry Marvin, she was shocked. She said, "Why would you marry a man with all those children?" Because I loved him, and I was marrying all of them.

Marvin knew much of my past in the beginning, and he always allowed me room to be myself. He has given me strength when I was certain I was a failure. He consoled me after my many mistakes.

The girls, though young when we were married, always had tons of self-confidence. Both Marvin and their birth mother were not people to back down. Nor are any of the girls. They will take control of any situation and have been my teachers and my mentors for many of these years—nearly 50 now. Thanks to all of you.

I love you all.

TABLE OF CONTENTS

Corner One: The Beginning 7
    1 8
    2 11
    3 15
    4 25
    5 29
    6 31
    7 34
    8 37
    9 42
    10 45
Corner Two: Trouble Ahead 50
    1 51
    2 54
    3 59
    4 64
Corner Three: Rehab: A Turn For The Better 68
    1 69
    2 72
    3 77
Corner Four: I've got it this time. I will see a happy ending for sure. 81
    1 82

2	85
3	89
4	95
5	100
6	105
Final Puzzle Piece	108
About the Author	111

CORNER ONE: THE BEGINNING

The first piece is always easy; I pick a corner.
Innocence. I have no idea what the world has in store
for me, but I'm ready!

1

The house on the hill is the first place I remember. It's 1951, I'm four and I'm poor, but do I know that? Of course not. I was very happy there with Mom and my brothers, Chuck and Eddie. It was a small house. We never used the front door or the living room. We lived in the kitchen. We would go through the back door. Outside at the corner was a galvanized tub to collect rain from the roof. That was our bathtub on Saturday, assuming it had rained that week.

Step into the kitchen with a wall on the left. You could look straight through to the living room. I could see the front door from here. It had a small, diamond-shaped window at the top. A set of stairs went up to the right, behind the wood stove. Mom would cook here, and it would heat the house all year. If she cooked, there would be heat. Opposite the stove was the sink with a hand pump to pull up the water. You must remember to prime the pump, or you'll have to go to the well and pull up enough water to fill a milk bottle. Next to that was a Formica table and an ice box. The iceman would bring in a big block of ice and put it in a box at the top. We had a milkman who would deliver milk. There was a bin outside; we would put the empty bottles in the bin, and he would replace them with full ones.

For the bathroom, we would use the outhouse during the day. For those not in the know, that would be the little wooden shed at the back of the house. It had a wooden bench with a hole in it to sit on, and newspapers or the old Sears catalog for wiping. At night I slept in the bed with Mom. We would use the honey pot, a porcelain pot that was under the bed, and in the morning, we would have to dump it in the outhouse. The boys slept upstairs. I never went up there; I don't know if there was a room or just the attic. They would carry a candle to go up there at night. No electricity of course.

Saturday was bath day. The boys would carry in the rain barrel and Mom would have the tea kettle boiling. I was the baby, so I got the first clean water. Eddie was next, then Chuck. Mom would sponge bathe at the sink.

I never knew my father; he was a soldier, and he didn't live with us. But Mom did have a friend named Len.

One day she said, "I have great news. Len wants to marry us, and we will be a family."

She said we were so lucky that he wanted all of us.

2

Moving on to the suburbs—we were looking for a new house.

"I think we found it," Len said, so we went to see the house.

But you could hardly see it, the house was covered with trees and lilac bushes. When we got to the back door it was locked. So, Daddy Len opened a window and said, "Nancy, I'm going to put you in the sink. Then you jump down to the floor and open the door."

I did, I saved the day. The house was big—I had never seen a house so big. We bought that house. It had a sink with hot and cold water. A refrigerator that needed no ice. An electric stove and lights that turn on at the wall. Upstairs there were three bedrooms and a bathroom with an indoor toilet I loved to flush. And the grandest was the big bathtub; it had hot and cold water too. No more sharing water. I had my own room and the boys shared another. Mom and Len had the third one.

In the cellar was a furnace to heat the house. The coal man would come over with a truck that had a big chute and would fill the bin in the cellar. Daddy Len or the boys would shovel the coal into the furnace. Now I knew that we had been poor because now we were rich. Daddy Len worked three jobs. He was a fireman, and he helped a local plumber. And on his days off, he sold Collier's Encyclopedia. He would use the money to turn that old house, which I thought was already beautiful, into a really nice place. He began tearing it apart, and we all helped to make it better. We all would have to work on these projects, except for Mom, who was the cook and clean-up crew. I helped build a built-in desk in the new living room. I was so proud; you would have thought I built it myself.

We had a new baby brother, Lenny. He was cute and Mom let me hold him. But he was sick when he came home from the hospital. He would scream and scream all day. But when Perry Comeau would sing on the radio, he would be quiet for 30 minutes. The doctor sent him back to the hospital. His bowels were all messed up.

They had to operate, and he was in the hospital for a long time. During that time the neighbors would bring him gifts—lots of gifts. The rest of us kids were jealous. I think we wished we could be sick too. But we were happy after he came home to stay.

The next year we had a new brother, Carl. I was going into first grade. Mom bought me a beautiful new dress. I was excited. But when I got up that morning, I had wet the bed. Mom was so mad.

She said, "Lay down on the bed."

She took my brother Carl's diaper and put it on me.

She said, "Only babies wet the bed. So, you're going to go to school wearing a diaper until you can stop wetting the bed."

I didn't know why I wet the bed. I couldn't help myself, I just did it. Lying in bed one night after that I knew I needed to pee, but I was afraid. I realized that I didn't want to go into the bathroom because Daddy would hear me. Then he would come into my room. I didn't like what he did. In the morning I told Mom why I wet the bed. It's because Daddy would come into my room at night and put his fingers in me. Now she was furious.

"How could you say such a thing about him? You must be imagining that. Don't you realize how lucky we are? He married us and gave us this beautiful house."

There, the trap was set. If I told, I would wreck our family. It would be my fault. She then told Daddy what I had told her. So later he said to me, "This is a special thing that daddies do with little girls they love so much. But we're not supposed to talk about it to anyone else."

3

First grade was fun; we would walk about a mile and a half to school. And next door to the school was Robert's Bakery—they made Hostess doughnuts, and they had a little store. We could buy doughnuts that weren't good enough to sell but were good enough to eat. Daddy continued to come into my room many nights. Now, if I was sleeping on my side, he would put his thing in my mouth. I really hated that. I told him to stop, and he said that if I told anyone no one would believe me. After all, I was just a kid. They will send you away to a reform school, he said, and you will never see your mother or your brothers again.

I am really scared now! I would pray hard. The boys and I would go to Sacred Hearts Catholic Church, because Mom was Catholic. Dad said he was a Home Baptist. We kids would play with the neighbors in the backyard. There were four houses and a huge yard between us. Lots of kids, but all the others went to Catholic school. I was kind of lonely. But in the third grade a new girl moved into the neighborhood, and she went to my school. Bunny became my best friend. From that day on we were almost always together. I would be at her house whenever I could. She had a great family. I loved her dad and mom. And she had two sisters, one older and one younger. Bunny's dad called me daughter number four. They were Italian and they had a big family. On weekends, the whole family would come over, plus me. Cousins, aunts, uncles, and Noni and Pop (which would be called Grandma and Grandpa in my house). And to me it seemed that they would start cooking at breakfast and cook all day. There would always be people at the table eating. And the food was delicious. Bunny and I joined Catholic Daughters, a church group that met each week. We were busy kids.

In our new house, we had a telephone. They were party lines; you could pick up the phone and an operator would answer. You tell her who you want to call, she'd say ok and plug into their phone. In order to know who the call was for, we had two rings; other neighbors had one and three.

The boys had a radio in their room. They loved to scare me. They would play *The Shadow* and *The Creaking Door*, radio shows that would tell scary stories with sound effects every night. They would play them really loud because they knew I hated to be scared. Before I would go to bed the older boys would run upstairs and wait for me. I knew they wanted to scare me. But every night I would tell myself, *This time, I won't be scared.* It didn't work, I was scared every time.

We had a black and white TV in the living room. As children we would watch *Howdy Doody* and we would drink our milk in a toast to the President of the United States, Dwight D. Eisenhower, Ike. His picture was on the wall, and the TV would play the president's song: *Hail to The Chief.* Again, as on the hill, I was certain we were rich. But we weren't; I remember going to the dump with Dad before Christmas one year. We picked up bicycle parts. We took them into the basement, and we built two whole bikes for Lennie and Carl. I remember painting them. The boys thought they were new bikes.

Mom was now on a bowling team, and they would

practice every Tuesday night. The big boys would go out with friends. The younger ones were in bed and that was the night that Daddy would make me touch his thing. Then he would make me put it in my mouth.

Our kid brother Lennie, who always cried as a baby, was now a fun kid. He turned out to be what we would call a smart ass—not one to follow the rules. He loved to push the limits. Growing up, I was Daddy's special girl, so I got off lightly. The baby, Carl, was so sweet and could do no wrong. Often the cellar door would open, and Daddy would reach in and take his marine belt off the nail. One-quarter inch of leather. He'd say, who did this or that? If we confessed, he'd say, "Pants down, lean over the chair," and he would give us four or five whacks. If no one would say, then smartass would get it, of course. And he would get it worse than any of us, because he would refuse to cry. That made Daddy mad.

Lennie was also a funny man. He would always make us laugh. Mealtimes were to be sacred at our house. Children did not talk. Children should be seen and not heard. Especially no laughter. But Lennie (smart ass) would start to tell a story, and we would think, *Oh lord, here it comes.* We knew he was going to make us laugh;

even Mom was scared. As the story would get funnier, we would be choking on our food, trying not to laugh. Daddy and Lennie would be staring at each other, stone-faced. We would all burst into laughter and Lennie would get it again as usual.

Speaking of mealtimes: Noon lunch and 5pm supper. Set in stone. You must empty your plates because they are starving in China. I once said we could mail it to them. That was a mistake, more laughter. It sounded reasonable to me. Every day, breakfast was cereal. School lunch was peanut butter and jelly or ham and cheese sandwiches. Maybe on weekends we would get Chef Boyardee. Only two cookies each for dessert. Every week there was the same menu: Wednesday was Prince spaghetti day; Friday was steak and mashed potatoes; Saturday was hot dogs and beans with fried dough. Always the same unless it was Christmas or Thanksgiving.

There was one Thanksgiving that Dad said, "Isabelle, do not buy a turkey. No one is going to tell me what I must eat. A man's house is his castle, and he rules. We will have oatmeal!" And we did.

When I was seven, we had two big hurricanes. Edna was first; we sat in the living room and watched the big oak tree swing back and forth. We thought it was going to come out of the ground, but it didn't. Then the second hurricane, Carol. The river had overflowed; it came almost up to our house. We wanted so badly to go out and play in the water. It was exciting. But Mom said no way, there were river rats that were running all over the streets. We had to stay in. It took a few days for the water to drain out of the street and then we went back to normal.

Sometimes on a hot weekend we would put on our swimsuits and walk past the papermill, down a long dirt road to the mill pond in the next town. It was a beautiful pond with a huge sand hill on one side and a rope swing on the other. On the way back, if it was ready, we would pick an ear of corn from the farm on the side of the road. At this same farm in the winter, there was a big depression in the cornfield that would freeze over. Kids from all over would come to ice skate. I loved to skate but hated the cold. That's about the time I began threatening to move to California as soon as I was old enough.

Bradford was a small town just across the river from Haverhill, a bigger city. Not like Boston or New York. But to me, it was a big city. There were lots of factories along the river—don't swim in the water because it's black. On one side of our house there was a big white house. The owners of the sawmill lived there. The sawmill was closer to the river, and there was a tannery right on the river, too. The tannery didn't smell very good. That's where they would take the leather and make it soft so that you could make clothing out of it. At noon every day, the sawmill would blow a big horn to say that it was lunchtime, and again at 5:00 p.m.—time for the shops to close. Every child in town knew that this was when you had to go home to eat.

We lived high on the hill; there was a little street between our house and the white house. Behind that house was a tower whose bottom was way down the hill at the sawmill. But at the top, which was on our side, there was a little door. That tower would often be filled to the top with sawdust. Heaven for us kids. We would open the door, jump in, and bounce around on all that sawdust. It was a lot of fun. Until Mom saw our clothes one day and knew what we did. "That's so dangerous, do not go in there again."

On weekends we would pull our little wagon around the neighborhood and fill it up with cardboard and newspapers, then down the street to the paper mill. They would put our wagon on a big scale and pay us for it. Big bounty, relatively speaking. Then we would go to one of the local family-owned markets, of which there were many, and we would buy penny candy. You could get a lot of candy for a nickel. Sometimes we would walk into our little town square. It had one market and a few stores. A pharmacy with a soda fountain where you could get a Vanilla Coke. There was a butcher's shop where you could buy meat. And a store called The Pickle Barrel where you could buy a pickle from the barrel. They'd wrap it in wax paper, and you could eat it as you walked along the street. The store we went to the most was at the corner—Zukies. They had soft ice cream and candy bars. And that was the place.

No mowing grass in our backyard. It connected with four other neighbors, so we had one huge backyard where all the kids would play all year round. There was nothing but dirt. Moms would sit in lawn chairs and watch us. We kids would play ball, swim in a blow-up pool, or just run around under the sprinklers and scream and shout.

On Saturdays we would go across the bridge to Haverhill. There was a big Woolworths store on the corner. First stop, roasted peanuts to bring to the movies. There were three theaters: The Strand, The Colonial, and the Paramount. If we were lucky, we could go to all three. Each had newsreels, cartoons, and a movie, sometimes in 3D. There were lots of stores here, and a bowling alley. On Sunday we would stay on our side of the tracks and go to Skateland to roller skate. After mass of course. Sometimes my brothers would make me go on the railroad bridge. When I complained they'd say, "We'll tell mom you wore lipstick at Skateland." Oh well, trapped again.

We got a movie projector and Dad would often rent a movie like Disney for us all to watch. One Tuesday when Mom was bowling, he brought down a different movie. He also had one of Mom's bras and garter belts with silk stockings. I didn't even have breasts—I may have been 10 years old. But he made me put them on, and he played this new movie. It was terrible. There was a woman doing all these things with a man and saying things I didn't understand. Daddy stopped the movie and made me say and do those things. Then he took out a Polaroid camera. It made instant pictures. He made me pose and he took pictures. When he was done, he showed them to me.

Then he said, "If you tell anyone I will show them these pictures. I will tell them what a bad girl you are, that you tempted me, and I couldn't resist. You will have to go to jail."

At 10 years old, why wouldn't I believe him? After that time, I believed that he was a very bad man, but what could I do? We had a little room by the attic stairs where Mom had a sewing machine. At night I would take the scissors and hold them in my hand under the pillow, hoping I would have the courage to stab him, and he would die. I never did, of course. I was afraid I would do it wrong and he wouldn't die all the way.

Now I am going into the fourth grade at a new school. During the first week the teacher said, "Nancy, I need you to go to the nurse's office."

I did, and when I got there, she asked me if I had a problem going to the bathroom. I said no. She said the teacher noticed that I would keep my hand in between my legs in class.

"Why would you do that? Is there something else you'd like to tell me?"

Did they know or suspect? I didn't want to go to jail.

4

In the summer we would drive to Searsport, Maine, to see Mom's mother. Oh, how I loved the farm. It was a small house with lots of land. Later I would learn it was about 200 acres. Behind the house was a mountain with blueberries and beehives. There was also an outhouse here. A couple of cows, a chicken coop, and what seemed to me a big garden. Grandpa would be up before the sun to do chores and go to work at Maplewood Poultry Factory. I would stay with Grandma, and we would sing. She had a record player and there was electricity here. She would play gospel music. My favorite was Tennessee Ernie Ford. May have been a cousin for all we know, Grandma had been a Ford before she married.

I remember making blueberry muffins. In the morning we would go milk the cows and put the milk in the refrigerator, then go get the eggs from the chicken coop and up the mountain to get the blueberries. In the kitchen, Grandma would pull out the special wood. You need different wood for different things, she would say. The wood would go in the baking section of the stove. Then we would get the sifter and get flour from the bin. We needed the sifter to keep the bugs out of the muffins; cut off a chunk of butter and we were on our way.

I remember one day when we were washing dishes (I was drying), Gram looked at me and put a finger over her mouth to shush me. Then she quietly opened the window. She opened a drawer in the kitchen, pulled out a gun, aimed out the window and BAM! Shot a deer. Now we'll have plenty of meat for this winter. Grandpa will dress it out when he gets home.

We didn't have heat or AC here, only the kitchen stove and a parlor stove. No heat in the bedrooms but we slept in a feather bed. And I do mean *in* the bed. You'd sink way below the bed's edges and with a down cover, it felt sort of like being in an oven.

Back home again. We would go to the YMCA after school, and they were starting a swim team. Bunny suggested that we go to tryouts.

I said, "Not me, I'm not a good swimmer."

"Ok," she said, "but come with me and watch me."

"Alright," I said.

There were a lot of girls there at the Olympic-size pool. They would call out a name you'd have to swim the length of the pool and back to make the team. A few girls made the team, most of whom we didn't really know well. They came from all over the city. Then they called my name. Oh no!

Bunny said, "Go ahead."

I told her I was afraid.

She said, "You can do it, I know you can."

I was too embarrassed to refuse so I jumped into the pool and started to swim. I swam like my life depended upon it. Because I believed it did. I just closed my eyes and swam until I hit the other end, took a deep breath and swam back. I did it! Bunny was so happy, but I was not. I was still scared. We both made the team, of course. The good thing was it meant one more night without having to see Daddy. Once again Bunny was my salvation.

It was about this time, at maybe 12 years old, that I started to get those breasts that all the other girls wanted,

The Pieces of My Life | 27

and I dreaded. And they were big, oh dear. At confession one Saturday I told the priest what Daddy was doing to me. He said there was nothing he could do to help me. You must pray and move out of the house as soon as you turn 18. So that was the plan. As I developed, so did Daddy's interest. Again, Bunny to the rescue. She signed us up for Girl Scouts. Another night away from home.

5

Haverhill was a shoe city, with many shoe factories, and they all had stores where they sold samples in my size; high-quality shoes to go to New York City. I had no idea that these shoes were worth a fortune; I just thought they were pretty and cheap.

I would also babysit for my aunt Beverly. That was wonderful. She had a record player and lots and lots of albums. After my cousins were in bed, I would play music and sing and dance. Here, my love of music was born.

Sometimes it's a relief to come home to anything that keeps Daddy's mind off of me. Like one evening, I came home to find Daddy fuming. It seems, as he was driving down the main street, he looked up at the pool hall above the stores and there was Lennie, the smart-ass, playing pool. Lennie was warned that Len was coming in. He went out the back door up the street and ran over the bridge, running out of his shoes and leaving them there. He stayed out very late to give Len a chance to cool down.

Now I'm in junior high school. Getting attention from some boys I can't date, and besides, I'm scared. I heard some say I had big breasts because I let boys play with them. Did Daddy do this to me? Now I hate him more.

I asked Mom if I could go to dancing school. She said yes. I loved it. Pretty dresses but Daddy was the shopper, and there was always an extra price to pay for that special dress. That was also where I tried my first cigarette. During the break a bunch of us would go out to the patio to talk and smoke. One puff and I said no way. But the deal was that each week one person would bring a pack. Then it was my turn. I bought the cigarettes and put them in my dresser. Mom found them and didn't believe I wasn't smoking until she made me smoke in front of her puff after puff. I was sick; if I had wanted to smoke before, that would have been the end.

6

High school, I made it. Once again Bunny jumped in. The Sacred Hearts Church was starting a theater group. They would do musicals each year. Bunny had convinced her dad that he had to play the lead in *The Desert Song*. He agreed, and they both said, Nancy, you need to be in the show too. This was great—there were lots of rehearsals late at night. Thank you, Bunny. Many years, *South Pacific*, as native girls. *The Sound of Music*, as nuns. *The King and I*, as the king's women.

I loved that I could be anyone but me. From then on, I found I could escape through music and dance.

Bunny was going to be a nurse, so I said, Me too. The school guidance counselor said No, Nancy, you'll never make it; you don't test well. How about going to X-ray school? Ok, what schools are there? There is one in

Gloucester that starts the first week in July. Perfect, I will get out of the house right after graduation. Tuition is not bad, and you can start getting paid even while in school. That's the one! It was a hospital-based program in Gloucester, Massachusetts: Addison Gilbert Hospital.

Career selected, I signed up for the future nurses' club, for all those seeking medical careers. On the 22nd of November of that year, while I was at a club meeting at Haverhill High School, there was an announcement over the loudspeaker that President Kennedy had been shot in Dallas. We went into the auditorium and watched the unbelievable news on a small TV screen. Everyone in the United States looked at things differently now. We had never had anything like this happen before. We heard that night that he had died. The Vietnam War, The Cuban Missile Crisis, and now our president dies. The happy days of the Fifties are surely over.

Mom was going to have another baby; I was kind of excited. She was huge, and when she went to the doctors, we found out why. She was having twins. Wow, two more babies. The babies were born on May 9th. Two girls—one died right after being born, and the other died in the hospital two weeks later. We never got to see them. After thinking a while, I thought that God had taken them early so Daddy wouldn't do to them what he did to me. Then I was glad because I wouldn't have been there to protect them.

7

It turned out that Bunny had applied to the same school. They also have a nursing program. We were both accepted and lived in the same dormitory. Good by Leonard! The nurses' residence was next to the hospital and there was an underground tunnel leading to it so that we didn't have to go outside in the winter. My room was on the third floor, second door across from the bathroom. It overlooked the parking lot where I could see my new car. Not really new of course, but it was mine. A cherry red '57 Chevy Impala with a white top and white leather seats. There was a fence between the hospital and the residence so no one could see it from the street.

I loved my classes and got good grades. It was a work-study program, so I was taking X-rays within a few weeks of starting. We had a real darkroom where we would develop the films. You had to watch the X-rays and when they looked good, you'd put them in the fixer to stop them from developing more, then put them in the dryer for 30 minutes. If the doctor needs it sooner, you take it out of the fixer to show him. That's why they say "wet reading;" the films were actually wet.

In a few months I could take calls; after hours, if someone needed an X-ray, I would be called back to the hospital. It paid only a dollar an hour, but it was for all night or all weekend. We would go to the hospital and take the X-rays while there was an actual tech who was on call too. But please do not call us, they said. The first weekend I was on call, I went to the hospital where they had brought in a little girl who was deceased. She needed a head X-ray. She had fallen out of a boat and her hair got caught in the motor blades. Her head was a mess, I don't know how I was able to contain myself. But this was now my job and I had to do it. I kept in touch with Mom to let her know when I would be home and tell her my plans for the week. After all, this was still the '60s—if you didn't call Mom at least once a week, she'd call the police to check on you.

One week when I had nothing planned a girl came

running upstairs and said my father was here. She said, "Wow, he's so handsome." He had told the housemother he wanted to surprise me and take me out to dinner.

I was shocked—how dare he! I didn't want to make a scene, so I said ok. When I got in the car, he said he had tickets to see Tony Bennet in the third row of a dinner club. What a dirty trick. But I went and was surprised that he didn't even try to touch me.

When we got back, he said, "We'll do this again."

I said, "Please don't."

Then he said, "I can take you now. I'll be your first and you'll love it, and no one can arrest me because you're 18."

I went back to the nurses' residence and told the house mother that if he ever showed up again to say that I had gone to stay with a friend. If he returned to the house after that, the house mother never told me. I was glad of that.

8

One of the nursing students and I went downtown once and met a couple of sailors. The Coast Guard had a buoy tender at the dock overnight. We had dinner and I asked, "Can we see the boat?"

They said sure, very proud of themselves. We went to the docks and indeed it was a nice craft. I said, "Let's go aboard."

"I don't think it's a good idea," one of them said.

The other said, "Why not? We'll just be quiet."

It was dark out and we had just tiptoed up the ramp and started to walk around when someone said, "Hey sailors, you back?" Oops! Fortunately, there was a little boat hanging inside the rail. We ducked under it. The boys talked for a few minutes, and we got off as soon as they left. A close call to say the least.

While at work one day, however, I did get a visit from my biological father. I had only seen him once in my life at that point. I was with a patient; he had a new wife who was a sheriff. They came into the X-ray department together; she had her hand on her pistol and told the staff to bring me to them. One of the staff took them to Dr. Wells, Chief Radiologist. The man said, "I'm her father and she must come to court to testify for me." Dr. Wells had them wait outside his office and called the darkroom phone.

"Do you know what this is about?"

"No, I'm not even sure he's my father."

Dr. Wells, only five feet tall, left his office. He told them to leave the hospital and never come back. I was scared. I went into the doctor's office and called Mom. She said she was indeed going to court today. My father was claiming that my mother was taking the money he sent her and he wanted it back. Mom said no, his money was paying the bulk of my tuition.

About two weeks later I received a package from Florida. It was from my father. In it were multiple pictures of me that had been in glass frames. They were all smashed. On top was a note saying, *You are not a daughter of mine!*

Our hospital and my residence is in the town of Gloucester, Massachusetts. Gloucester is a fishing town and there is a beautiful waterfront with a sea wall. When there was a big storm, we would drive down there to stand beneath the crashing waves. What a thrill! On Halloween they had the Horribles Parade. People would wear costumes and the children would decorate their bikes. At Christmas I went home, but no problem—the whole house was too busy. New Years' back in Gloucester for the blessing of the fleet, the biggest event of the year for a fishing town.

A friend from the nursing school was dating a boy from town. One night she said he had an older brother and asked if I would like to go to the movies with them. Sure, although he was quite a bit older than me. Daddy's age. I liked him; his name was Fred. He said he'd ask me out but didn't have a car. I told him I'd pick him up.

We then had a few more dates. One night we were at a little beach talking, and we then decided to go into the back seat. We started necking and it was kind of exciting. I had never done anything like that before. I let him touch me like Daddy did. But this was different; I liked it. I dropped him off and went back to the nurses' residence. I parked the car and went through the back door and upstairs to my room. As I began to undress, I realized my clothes were stained with blood—lots of blood. I took my clothes and went into the shower. There I washed myself and my clothes. I went to bed shocked that I was no longer a virgin; I hadn't felt a thing. I guess I just really didn't know that this was how that sex thing worked. I just did what came naturally. I'm certain he had no idea I was a virgin either. Probably why he never called again.

That wasn't my only shock. When I woke up early the next morning as I always did, I looked out the window and down at my car. The white leather back seat was covered with blood. I wet a towel and ran downstairs to clean it up before anyone else could see. Thankfully I didn't get pregnant.

At Christmas that year I received a Ouija board. We began playing it at night. Everyone loved it, it was such fun. Until one night the board told us that we would have a man come into the dorm. That night, a disoriented patient had left his room, found the tunnel, and came into the dorm. Next morning the place was buzzing. The girls told the housemother that they knew, because I had predicted it! She was livid—"Ok Nancy, it's you or that board, one of you must go."

"Ok, I'll take it home." I think they believed I made the man come over.

9

As student techs we would work all summer, and in the fall we began our second year. Our classes would be in Boston at Northeastern University. The hospital had a contract with a woman who ran a rooming house close to the school. The first week I drove my car with two other girls. In that week alone I got four parking tickets. I had to take the subway to Roxbury to pay the fines. From then on, we took the train.

That done, we settled in. Three of us shared a room on the first floor. Upstairs were two Japanese boys. One was a dental student, the other a salesperson for FujiFilm. We hadn't used this film in the X-ray department yet, but soon we would. The boys would cook for us, a great deal, since in our room there was only peanut butter, jelly, and crackers. After school we would often take the subway to Boston Gardens and go shopping, always in the basement stores. It wasn't until months later that we realized the 40 minute subway ride was unnecessary—we could have walked it in 20 minutes.

I went to a frat party with a boy I met in school named Dave Tibbets, another first and only for me. That appeared to be my MO, never dating anyone for long. Until Eric Ruderman. He was special; we were never romantic, just great friends. We would go to bars and sing, dance, and play pool. Then we'd spend hours talking. We talked about the Vietnam War. We had both taken part in a sit-in protest on Northeastern's steps. We would talk about politics and religion. He was Jewish and his parents kept a kosher home. I was intrigued when he didn't try to convert me.

He said, "We don't do that. We believe that your faith is a relationship between you and your God. If you have a good relationship with Him, you're good."

We would remain friends for years until his passing in 2000. While at Northeastern we were required to take an X-Ray Physics class. I had already taken this class at the hospital school. After the first test, while sitting in the student union, a couple of girls from other schools asked how I could have aced the test. They hadn't understood anything the teacher was saying. The teacher was a nuclear physicist from MIT and was talking way over their heads. So, I began a class in the student union. The program director found out and came to class. Told me I had to stop. The other girls said no way, if Nancy stops, we'll never pass any tests. So I was allowed to continue. That teacher didn't return the next semester.

10

Graduation 1967

Well, graduation was here; I had been accepted for a new job at Danvers State Hospital. They were opening a new school for handicapped children in September. I had taken the civil service X-ray exam. It was more difficult than the registry for X-ray technologist, but I received the third highest grade in the state.

Meanwhile, the local newspaper had printed our graduation pictures. I got a letter shortly after from the USS Intrepid saying that they had had a contest. All the boys took their local papers and chose the girl from graduation photos that they would most like to come home to. Then they all voted on one, and it was me! The boy from Gloucester who submitted my picture came to meet me. He was cute and told me that he was a twin. We had a nice visit, but we would both be moving so that was our only time together.

Now I had to move out of the dorm so the new students could come in. My new job didn't begin for three months. I went back home and was greeted by Leonard, no longer Daddy to me.

He said, "If you come back to my house, you will get a job."

Of course, no one wanted to hire me for three months. But I was able to find work at the local bakery. It was the night shift, 10 p.m. to 6 a.m. My job was to sort the bread and rolls as they came along the conveyor. We would look for anything that didn't look right; they were called crips, like crippled.

Most of the others on the line were Dominicanos. But we had a great time. Each night, one of us would bring in a pound of butter. It would stay on the counter. When the belt would stop, we'd pull out our favorite crips, load them with butter, and enjoy. My favorites were the egg rolls. At the end of three months the owner said, "Please stay. You work hard and the others love you." Sorry, I have a career waiting for me.

New hospital, new nurses' residence. The hospital was awesome, it was all built from stone and looked like a castle. It sat way on top of a hill; you could see it for miles. Directly across from the main building was the medical building. I would be working there, in the basement next to the morgue. The new nurses' residence was next door.

The Chief X-Ray Tech, Ed, was wonderful, but there were rules. I was only to X-ray the children. Besides, you're moving too fast. Slow down, there's plenty of time. Hard for me as I was always a mover. The X-ray techs were girls, and we would call him Dad because he always sounded like one.

The Pathologist, Dr. Baxter, was a little different. He would let cheese ferment in his refrigerator and when it was good and green, he would eat the green part, then replace it to get green again. He said it's healthy. Penicillium, you know. Maybe he was right. He also carried around a urinal, the portable kind they use for hospital patients in bed. He would drink from it. He said it had tiger juice in it to give him energy. I don't think anyone knew what he was drinking. When X-Ray was not busy, I would often go in and watch him perform the autopsies. He would sometimes bring us a brain from one of the deceased patients and we would inject it with Barium. We would then take X-rays of it, so we could see any abnormalities. Perhaps it would help in the diagnosis of certain mental conditions later. A Cat Scan does this now.

My life now revolved around this new job. We could eat in the cafeteria, open to staff and patients alike. Occasionally we would drive to the bottom of the hill. There was a diner down there. One day we girls had just finished lunch. I said watch this, and I told the waiter that Dad was paying for our lunch, pointing to Ed. We hurriedly left but when we got out, I realized I had left my keys on the table. I went back in; Dad was holding up my keys. I took the keys and he said loud enough for everyone to hear, "Fifty dollars!" The joke was on me.

Next to the diner was a bar, The Harp and Bard. It was an Irish Pub with singing bartenders. I felt at home here, Mom being Irish. And across the highway was a shopping center on one side. On the other side was Putnam Pantry where you buy a scoop or two of ice cream and they had a bar of toppings, oh my goodness. Everything you could think of was there and you could put on as much as your dish could hold. Small dishes of course, but what a treat.

On Saturday nights the hospital would have a dance for the patients. Staff were encouraged to go to chaperone and mingle with the patients. I love music and dance. I went every Saturday. As the weather got cooler I danced with a new patient named Mickey. He resembled Fagin from the musical *Oliver*.

CORNER TWO: TROUBLE AHEAD

1

Mickey told me that he would check himself into the hospital every fall and they would release him in the spring. I would later realize the game: he was a heroin addict. By fall, when he was out, he would need more and more drugs, and it was getting expensive. Heroin is a downer, a drug that relaxes you. At the hospital they would wean him off the heroin using uppers or speed. So, in the spring, he would start over needing very little heroin.

Speaking of fall, I was falling in love, big time. We spent much of the winter together at the dances, having meals together and going for walks on the grounds. The campus was huge, and Mickey was a low-risk patient, so he was allowed to go anywhere on the hospital grounds.

There were some locked units and there were many seriously scary patients here. Even many of the guards were scary. We used to say you have to look at their belt—if they had a huge ring of keys, they were a guard. If not, watch out.

We had one patient named Bobby, the first person I knew who was gay. Bobby would come by the department and ask if he could touch our faces.

He would say, "I wish I could have girly skin like you have, so soft and smooth." And he was so sweet. One morning, we came into work and found Bobby passed out on the floor in front of the X-ray room. We helped him up and brought him in. "I have such pain down here," he said.

Ed took Bobby's pants off to find that his testicles were the size of a grapefruit. So we X-rayed his pelvis to see what was happening. Bobby said he had tied a shoelace around his scrotum. After taking much time to get the shoelace off, we asked him what happened.

He said, "I asked Mr. Chang why he only had hair on his chin." Mr. Chang, a patient who was over 100 years old, had a Fu Manchu beard.

"He told me that his mother would squeeze his testicles every day as a child, and that stopped his hair from growing. So," Bobby said, "I figured I was starting late. That's why I tied the shoelace to speed things up."

I would still meet up with Eric a couple times a month. He was always my friend. We would go to Sandy's Nite Club where we could watch people and dance a little. I came home to the residence one night and was told by the house mother that Leonard was asking for me. Oh no! He will never stop. I spoke with another priest. He asked for the details of what had been done to me. I said forget it. No way I'm telling him. I think he just wanted to hear the details. He seemed pleased to be asking such pointed questions. I can't believe I'm still trapped.

2

The weather had broken, and Mickey was leaving. He said, "Why don't you come to Dianna's with me?"

Sure, this was the real thing. Dianna had a nice home in Beverly Farms. She lived there with her son Burt and various other people like Mickey and me. She was about our age; Burt was maybe eight.

Up until now I had never taken any drugs or had more than a drink or two in a day. But often a group would congregate at Dianna's and smoke pot. I tried it a couple of times, but I really didn't like the feeling of being out of control, so my relationship with pot was limited.

Dianna had a big yard, and she and some of
the guys would go out back and shoot cans off a log. I said I could shoot so she let me use her rifle. I wasn't a

sharpshooter, but I wasn't bad. Better than some of the boys.

Among the regular visitors were Ray and Lita. Lita stayed with the pot crew. Ray didn't, so we began to talk. He, too, didn't like being out of control.

"I prefer meth," he said. "Want to try some?"

Ok. He pulled out a little packet of white powder. He showed me how he would wet his finger in his mouth and dip it in the bag. As we talked, I felt smarter. Now this I could do.

They were back again the next day, and he offered me another hit. We went outside and worked in the yard. I had so much energy. It was great. The next day was Monday and we all had to go to work. I went to work and was now looking forward to seeing Ray next weekend.

We all had good jobs. I really think all the fuss about drugs is kind of crazy. Ray was a factory manager, Lita was a teacher, and Mickey was a hair stylist. I told them that I had wanted to be a hairdresser and had worked in a home salon for two years. Leonard had said I was copping out by going to beauty school. You're too stupid to go to college! I loved doing hair and working at

Angie's salon. I had enough of Leonard saying I was stupid. I will prove him wrong. That was when I went to the guidance counselor. I would show him! So, I went to college. I was successful and happy, but I still loved doing hair. In fact, Lita had very fair skin and a dark, afro-style hairdo. She complained once that it was so hard to manage. I asked if I could try something. She said yes, do anything. I separated her hair and began at the top. Her once six-inch afro became two inches. As I got to the sides, I left the parts in front of her ears long, and in the back, I did the same. No one had seen a style like this before. Everyone liked it. Lita loved it! Now the sides and back were soft and curly, perfect for her petite body.

After a couple of weeks, I asked Ray if I could buy a bag of meth. The first bag lasted a month; then it was every week. I had no idea that I was beginning a long, difficult journey. And would not be able to change it.

Life with Mickey was idyllic. I was so happy. The sex was out of this world. Eric came to see me a couple of times at Dianna's but he wouldn't stay. He was just checking on me. He's unhappy with what's going on—"I'm here if you need me."

One day Mickey says it's time to go back. Where? To

the hospital, it costs too much to stay high. So, we left Dianna's, and I went back to the residence.

Now there's no more Mickey, no more sex. Just me, my job, and methamphetamine. I still meet up with Ray to buy meth. One day I woke up, looked in the mirror. My pupils are the size of saucers. I've been told that Dr. McNichol can help. I ran across the street and upstairs to his room. I'd never been there until now. It's a massive room in one of the turrets. In the center is an equally massive bed.

The doc looks at me and says, "Oh dear. Sit down here."

As I sit, he goes under the bed where he has many boxes. He pulls one out and it's filled with pills. A literal pharmacy. He says, "Here, take these and stay here for another 15 minutes." Crisis averted.

It's the end of the year and all files and X-rays over three years old need to be purged. The old X-rays go back to a company that pulls the silver back off the film and pays the hospital for it. So, we start putting paper in boxes and films in bins. The staff goes home for the weekend. But I live here, so a couple hits of meth and I dig in. Monday morning Ed comes in. He's incredulous, how can this be? It usually takes us a week to do this. I stayed all weekend. You better slow down Nancy.

I would often meet Eric at Sandy's to dance and shoot pool. We still talked a lot about religion. His religion made more sense, better than mine. Just a relationship between you and God. Simple, you and God. No buildings or elders, just you and him. I wonder if God even knows me?

3

Spring again; we go back to Dianna's. I'm so happy I have Mickey back. Many of the same people are here. A new guy, big Mike, is here, a giant. There's also something new, Black Ganja. Hashish that we smoke from a water pipe.

I do this now because it slows me down a little from the speed. We also do cocaine occasionally, usually before sex. The big thing is that we have bought tickets to the Woodstock Folk Festival. Everyone's excited. I made plans at work to take a week off, so we could go early and get a good spot. We would be going in a VW bus driven by a guy who I later understood was instrumental in the building of the Alvin Submarine.

A new girl showed up at the house. Her name was Susie, and she was a costume designer for shows in Boston's theater district. She looked like Twiggy: thin, no boobs, boy haircut. I only met her once. No biggy. It was about two weeks until Woodstock and we were making final plans.

Mickey came to me and said, "By the way, I'm moving in with Susie."

I was shocked beyond belief that he was leaving Barbie to be with Twiggy. I really didn't understand. That was it, I never saw him again. I'm certain he was at Woodstock but not with our group. I was still going. I was a big girl. We set out for New York on Tuesday so we would be early. We weren't the only ones, the highways were jammed. Everywhere we stopped there were heads going to Woodstock.

When we were getting close, the traffic slowed. By the time we reached the farm it was hardly moving. We were now on a single lane dirt road; traffic was so slow that only the drivers stayed in the cars and the rest of us walked. It was incredible so many people. We walked ahead and there was another VW bus with open sides. It looked like a candy store but was filled with pills. Some guys were handing out samples. Here try the pink ones, they're great.

What the hell, I'm alone at Woodstock. So I took it. Now, Mickey was no longer on my mind. It was over an hour before we had to stop walking. I guess this is where we camp. We pulled out the tents and were able to set up on the left side of the road. There was a hill on the right. After we set up, we found the path to the bowl where the concert was going to be held.

It was still three days to start time and already there were people lying on blankets. Someone from our group went to get some. We scouted a spot just to the left of center stage, about 10 blankets back. Great spot. A couple people sat on the blankets, and we went back to finish setting up camp. After setting up I noticed our neighbor, an absolutely gorgeous man, alone. So I introduced myself. "I'm Atilla," he said. "I'm from New York City." A Greek god, I was sure. We spent the night together.

The next morning, I was on blanket duty and remained there for the duration. I would not miss a show. This was my time, and I would take it all in. The place was incredible, it was created just for this day. We had walked up a hill through the woods to get to the top of this huge grassy bowl. Down again to the enormous stage. It was still two days before the start and there must have been over a thousand people already. I would never realize the scope of it until after I got home.

To the right of the stage was the first aid station. I could see it now but soon it would be hidden by the thousands of people that were about to be there. In any other place but here I would have stood out, but this was Woodstock. Everyone was unique. I wore well-worn wide denim bell bottoms. The bottoms were cut off and frayed. Had to be cut as I'm only 5'2". Lita likes to paint so before we left, she got out her paint. When she was finished my breasts were two huge daisies with my nipples as the center, two green stems down to my belly button, and two large green leaves coming out of them. I must have had a top somewhere, but I don't remember wearing it. Even when it rained, we just had a couple of umbrellas. Just wrap up in our blankets and sit back down.

Ritchie Havens was the first act, not my favorite but who cared. Just seeing all these people was a trip of its own. Everyone was moving, singing, dancing, or just walking. I was not a Ravi Shankar fan before, but his performance was incredible. The later acts had to be flown in by helicopter as the roads were now parking lots. Who had I come to see? Joan Baez who was at her best. Janice Joplin rocked the place. With Arlo Guthrie and Creedence Clearwater I just sang and danced. I was out of my mind with joy. Then Janice had the whole crowd screaming.

The place was undulating. It seemed like it was now a living thing. Or it may have been some of the pills I was given by my neighbors. I remember Joe Cocker and Jimmy Hendrix, he was the last. No hurry to get home, nothing could move until the first cars left. We all went down to the creek. The water was freezing but felt great. We were filthy, I just got in jeans and all. The only clothes I had with me anyway. Most people took it all off. We just laughed and screamed and splashed, like a bunch of very big children.

Afterward, we dried off and packed up. We began another very slow ride off the farm. Toward the end, the local firefighters were out holding their boots asking for donations. Those of us with money were generous. The townspeople were great; they were cheering us on as we left.

My one-week vacation was way past. Work understood—they knew where I had been and just wanted stories. Now I could see on the news what I had been a part of: history.

4

I go back to work. Now, being in a group of users, I can get meth from anyone in the group. So I see very little of Ray and Lita. Embarrassed about losing Mickey to Twiggy. A couple of weeks after returning from Woodstock, I realized my breasts were larger and painful. And my flat tummy was not so flat. It couldn't be, after nearly two years with Mickey. Still not believing I could be pregnant, I went to the pharmacy and picked up a pregnancy test. Positive. I was indeed pregnant. I was thrilled to be having Mickey's baby. But without Mickey I was confused about what to do next.

I was on my way to Gloucester to share my good news with friends. I began to get bad cramps. Pulled over to one of the small beaches. I had on a bathing suit and a long skirt. I thought maybe the cool water would help me. I took off my skirt; it felt good. I then sat on a rock.

The cramping had stopped and then became worse. The baby was coming—I couldn't stop it. It was not one, but two babies. Twin boys. I washed them off and held them in my arms. I named them David and Daniel, my favorite Bible names. I knew they were not alive but I just held them and cried. Afterwards I let the tide take them out. I never told anyone about them before writing this book.

Now I'm more depressed, losing the twins was probably the worst thing that had ever happened to me. I am wracked with guilt. Had I not gone to Woodstock and taken all those extra pills, might they have lived? Did I kill my babies? If I had the babies I would have had a reason to live. Now I have nothing. I'll go back to work but for what, I don't know.

I hadn't taken any acid since Woodstock. But now I would start tripping out of the blue. I remember walking past cars and having to jump away because I would see the grills open and try to bite me. Now I'm frightened of everything getting acid flashbacks.

One day the hospital director came into the X-ray department asking for me. He said, "I can't say it was you, but someone broke into our pharmacy last night and stole a large quantity of drugs. Might it have been you?"

Of course not. I couldn't believe it, I'm in a nuthouse filled with crazy people, and they think I robbed the pharmacy. Now they'll want to fire me. That was it! After work I planned on how I could commit suicide. Nothing to live for.

Looking around my room, I figured that if I opened my window and backed up against the door I could just dive onto the sidewalk. No chance of surviving. Ok, I'll do it. I opened the window, backed up against the door, and was slammed across the room. There were Ray and Lita.

"We were having dinner," Ray said. "We felt the Lord tell us you were in trouble, and we had to go now."

Now it was me who was nuts. Was I tripping again?

"How did you get past the housemother?"

"There was no housemother," Lita said, as she packed me a bag. They took me back to their home. On the way they told me they no longer do drugs.

"We have found the Lord. He led us to you."

I told them my plan and they said, "See? He wanted to save you."

"What are you talking about?"

"Jesus Christ, He's given us a new life. We want to help you."

I stayed at their home for maybe two more months. When I went back to the hospital, I got my car and my clothes. I don't even think I quit my job. I just left.

I was still using speed and they knew it but did not pressure me. They tried to get me to go into a program. I said no way.

CORNER THREE

Rehab: A Turn For The Better

1

One day Ray said, "We're going on vacation to the White Mountains for a few days. Want to come?" Of course. So, we were off. We ended up in Whitefield, New Hampshire, at The House of Hope. Ok, I figure, they pray every day at home, so what's different about this place? We got our rooms and there were lots of people there. Nice meals from the kitchen and a prayer service in the living room after dinner. We stayed Friday and Saturday. There was a church service on Sunday with a special preacher, Clinton White. They say he was a healing preacher. But he said, "Jesus heals, not me. He just uses me."

I liked him. After the service, Ray and Lita sat me down and told me that I was staying here. I was dumbstruck. How could they do this to me? They said, "You need this; you will thank us."

Then they left, and now a whole group of people stood around me. "We were all addicts and this program helped us. You'll get better, we promise."

Monday was indeed a new day, no drugs. Breakfast was easy, and before lunch I was told I'd be working in the kitchen. What? Everybody must work here, it helps with your withdrawal.

I would be making pudding for dessert. How hard could that be?

Hard enough, there would be about 15 people here. They handed me a huge pot and some boxes of pudding mix. They showed me around the kitchen, and I was on my own. I could do the math, each box serves six so I used three boxes. Add the milk, heat, and stir. But it didn't say to stir deep in the pot. I began serving and realized the bottom was all black.

"I'm sorry, no pudding tonight, I made a mistake."

"No, we'll serve it, and no one will complain. We all make mistakes. We forgive each other." Lesson one. Everyone ate it and there were no complaints. I asked if there might be another job for me, far from the kitchen.

"How do you feel about animals?"

I love animals. "Kenny can use some help at the Zoo."

A zoo? Oh yeah, I'm in.

It was a small zoo but there were quite a few different animals. This was a great move for me. Not only did I love it, but my body aches far exceeded my withdrawal symptoms—or perhaps they were all mixed together.

It wasn't long after that I asked Jesus to be my savior. I now believed that He had sent me here. I actually felt like a new person. They say born again. Yes, that's how it felt. At the zoo I especially liked the lions, they were so beautiful yet so scary. There was a hippo named Gracie, and we loved to feed her. Hold up a head of cabbage and her mouth would open wide. Basketball for us and dinner for her. Then there was the ocelot, who looked like a kitten with a big head. Kenny said to never ever hold on to her food when you feed her. He took an animal leg the size of my arm, held it up, and dropped it in her cage. Less than a minute and the bone was clean. She will clean your arm if it's nearby. Lesson learned; you don't need to tell me twice.

2

It was the beginning of summer; I was released from treatment. But I had nowhere to go. There was a small cottage on the property that one of the workers lived in alone, and I was offered the extra room. I was able to get a job less than a mile away at the Spalding Inn. This was a first-class resort where guests would book rooms for weeks at a time. I had plenty of experience working in restaurants during my college years, but I had never been to a place like this. China plates, crystal glasses. People would order a two-and-a-half-minute egg. We had a machine for that. We placed sterling finger bowls and fresh towels on the tables after each meal for our guests to wash.

In my first week working there was a lot of whispering. They said, "You're the new girl, but we'll let you take this guest. He's rich."

J. Paul Getty was indeed rich, and I was prepared to receive a large tip at the end of the week. Like all the guests, he was fussy. I made certain that everything was perfect for him. But at the end of the week his tip was the worst I'd ever gotten. I told the other servers and they laughed; he never leaves a good tip. The cheapest guy we know. He comes here every year. There is a far more expensive place just down the road, but he stays here because it's cheaper and then meets his friends at the Mountain View Lodge where he can play golf and bocce ball and not have to pay. Another lesson learned. Next year the new girl will have the pleasure.

At the end of the season, the Spauldings invited me to work at their Florida resort. I declined, but my roommate had a twin sister, Julie, who lived in Salem, Massachusetts, and was looking for someone to share expenses. Being familiar with the area, I accepted. It was a nice duplex near downtown. I worked more waitressing jobs. One day a young girl showed up at our door and asked if we had seen our neighbor, who was also our landlady.

"No, she's gone for the summer."

"Oh no, she's my aunt and my father sent me out here

to stay with her for a month."

We found out that Georgi was from LA, and was only 10 years old. Her father had put her on a plane with a few dollars and here she was. I invited her in and asked for her dad's phone number. He answered immediately. He said that he was unable to take her back until the end of the month. Would I kindly take care of her for that time? Of course not! What would I do with a child? But there was no alternative; she stayed for the month.

At first, she was very entertaining. She would sit in a chair at the table and immediately put both her feet behind her head. It's comfortable, she said. One day we went to a local park and Georgi fell off the swing and broke her wrist. Off to the local hospital where I had to fight to get her treated. After speaking with her dad on the phone, they agreed. After Georgi went home, Julie was to be going as a missionary somewhere in Europe. She would be leaving soon, and I could not afford to stay at the duplex alone.

I had been going to a Union Mission in Beverly. The building was owned by the pastor. It had an apartment upstairs that was in disarray, but I was told I could stay there if I liked. So I moved in, no hot water, and someone had left the attic window open. So my first job was to evict the pigeons. After work I would spend most of my time patching and painting, and soon the place looked pretty nice.

One day there was a guest minister preaching. He liked my testimony and said he could get me into a bible school. You'd make a great minister, he said. Indeed, the next year was spent in Lima, New York, at Elim Bible College, back in another dormitory. I truly felt that this could be my future, though I had many disagreements with staff and others. Why, if they were followers of Jesus Christ, were they not doing what he had asked of them?

Of course, this was Eric speaking again. He'd say, "We don't bring money to shul." Jesus had kicked the money changers out. And no selling of goods and animals. So why do we have collections at churches? And why do we have bingo and bazaars? One of us does not understand. He even said we didn't need the High Priests in the temple because we could now go directly to the Father. Rabbis today don't even give you answers. They will tell you to read the scriptures and then you can pray, and get the answer that's for you.

I did finish my training, however, and was scheduled

to go on a medical mission to Cameroon. All kinds of shots. Be careful of drinking water, always ask for a hot drink so the water is boiled. And never show your ankles, it is frowned upon by the natives. Long skirts or dresses with socks would be in order. A few weeks before we were to go, a war broke out in Africa, and the port of Lagos, where we had planned to travel from, was closed. School was over, and I was now an ordained minister with no job. Back to the Beverly mission.

3

The first place I gave testimony about my conversions was in Salem. After I spoke, a gentleman came up to me. "I'm Doctor Snell, and I'd like to hire you. Do you still have your radiology license?"

"I do, but I'm not sure you can hire me."

"Of course I can, everyone deserves a second chance. I'm a radiologist at Winthrop Community Hospital."

I was now a reverend but had no job to pay the bills, so I accepted. I had never believed I'd be able to work in X-ray again. Thank you, Lord!

This time the hospital had a little house next door where I would have a room. It took a bit of getting used to as the hospital was at the end of a runway for Boston's Logan Airport, so every time a plane would take off, the windows would rattle. But after a week I could truly say,

"What noise?"

This was another great time for me. I was to learn that Dr. Snell rode a motorcycle in good weather. Not just any motorcycle, but a BMW. It honestly looked like a cow to me. It was huge. I was asked to be a guest minister at a new church. As I walked up to the front, I saw a massive Star of David above the door and the words *Faith Temple.* Am I in the wrong place? It turned out it had been a synagogue and was now owned by an independent gospel church. Independent indeed. Eric is speaking to me.

During the holidays I went home to learn that Mom and Leonard were moving to Arizona where his sister had moved a few years prior. His mother was going with them, too; at the time she was renting one side of the duplex next door. Carl wanted to stay here with his friends and girlfriend. I had been notified that there was a job opening at Haverhill Radiology. It was mine if I wanted it. Mom suggested that Carl and I rent Grandma's place next door. I agreed. A couple of months before they were due to leave, Mom's mother unexpectedly came down from Maine. She had sold her place to the young man next door and wanted to go with them to Arizona. With us having a full house, she was able to rent a small place across the street. So, the plans were made. I gave my notice at Winthrop and took the job at Haverhill Radiology near the duplex.

When I got back home, Len's mother, Grandma Hall, was in our old house, which was now sold, and there were boxes everywhere. Carl and I moved into the duplex. The move was to be the next day. Carl and I went across the street to check on Mom's mother. She was on the floor. I, who was in the medical field, froze. Carl said, "Nancy, call for an ambulance." Operator, send an ambulance. Grandma had had a stroke. She went to the hospital unable to move so she had to stay here.

The rental truck was on its way to Phoenix. Grandma Noon was now in a nursing home. So I was in charge. For months, I would go from work to the home to have my lunch and feed Gram. She hung on for months. On Thanksgiving Day I was late getting to see her, and she died before I got there.

Feeding Carl was a different story. I should have asked for a meal allowance. Each morning he would have six eggs and a quart of milk. Also, half a bag of Oreos after every meal with more milk. He also played on a hockey team. His team's ice time was 11 p.m. After, he'd come home with the team in tow to get a snack. It sounds like I'm complaining. I'm not, he was a great kid, and I loved every minute of our being together. We lived there together until after Carl's graduation and his wedding. Then I was alone again.

CORNER FOUR

I've got it this time. I will see a happy ending for sure.

1

My brother Eddie was active in the local Yacht Club. We would often meet there and have dinner and maybe a drink. There was usually some weekend entertainment.

On one such visit he introduced me to Dick, a guy who lived nearby. He was good-looking, and he had been a pilot in the Korean War. We began to date—he was the perfect gentleman. Flowers, candy, cards. We'd see movies and listen to music. He never pushed me to go to bed. He must really love me; I'd never had a guy who wasn't after my body. I met his family and loved them all. He was the baby of the family, and they were happy to see us together. His parents had a huge house near ours, with a big backyard with a garden in the back that his mother tended diligently. His father had opened a local pharmacy. His brother and sister now ran it; his dad had had a stroke and, though wheelchair-bound, he maneuvered quite well. Dick and I talked about getting married. He said, "I was married once before very briefly. But because I was married in the catholic church I can't be married in the church."

So, we planned a small wedding with the justice of the peace. One of his sisters, Betty, was a nurse, and we would often go to her home. She and her husband would be our witnesses. There would be no big wedding, his dad was housebound and his siblings were much older than him. But I didn't care. I was so happy. The Justice of the Peace officiated and my new brother- and sister-in-law took us out to a nice restaurant afterward. After, we would be going on our honeymoon. Dick had it all planned. We would be going to Provincetown, Massachusetts, on Cape Cod. I had never been there, so I was excited. We arrived at a small little hotel.

I had dressed for bed in something sexy. He came to bed and said, "What a coincidence, this is the same room Annie and I had."

Who was Annie? He said, "My first wife."

"You took me to the same hotel where you took her?"

"Yes, we had our honeymoon here, too."

I was so shocked I couldn't even cry. Then he said,

"I'm too awake to sleep now. I'm going for a walk." When he returned, he crawled into bed beside me and made no advances. The rest of the honeymoon was the same. As was our married life. I was incredulous. What had I done? Perhaps this was God's way of punishing me for all I'd done wrong. I will wait and see. I firmly believed that marriage was forever. I would not break my vow.

When we got back home, I went back to work. He also went back to work at Gulf Oil where he was a truck driver. Long hours, good pay. Pretty normal in every way except in the bedroom. I was to take care of the budget. Ok, but the paychecks did not come home regularly. He would usually cash them and bring home what was left.

We would often go to the Yacht Club or the Elks Club. I rarely drank, since I would get drunk on two of anything. I'd rather dance and sing. He drank a lot more than he should have, but it didn't seem to affect him. When we got home, he would pass out. On a few occasions, he would be late coming home and I would go out the front door to find him asleep on the porch, not in a chair but on the deck. I would now realize he could drink a fifth and two six-packs and appear perfectly normal. Then he would pass out cold.

2

I was tired of renting; I wanted to buy a place. "No," he said, "I like renting." I kept looking and found a place in Kingston, New Hampshire. I said I'm buying it, you can come or not, I don't care. He came. I loved it, a small mobile home on a big lot. It had an addition on the back that looked across the street to Powwow Pond. Great little fishing and boating pond.

Dick wanted a Basset Hound. I loved dogs, so we bought Bridi's Ironsmith, a purebred basset hound pup. Smitty, we called him, or Mr. Smith. He was great company and security. If someone tried to break in, I wouldn't have to use the shotgun, his howl would scare anyone. He sounded enormous, and turned out to be pretty darn big later. 86 pounds. But because I held him as a puppy, he still believed he was a lap dog. We then bought him a mate, Samantha, and I began raising puppies. They were always house dogs, but we had a large, fenced pen in the back with a doghouse.

Things were settling down; I was now buying my home. I began working pretty quickly, painting and decorating. I put a Heatilator fireplace in the back room, then built faux stone surrounding it. It was beautiful; this was now my favorite room. Next, I put in a large, oval-shaped, above-the-ground pool.

Kingston was a great little historic town. Lots of old homes and buildings. In the center of town, Main Street split near the State Park entrance. Between the two roads was a wide grassy area like a park. It was called the Plains. Indeed, it was used as a park for all kinds of events. The school football team would practice here. The center was wide, with a road through the middle connecting the two roads, and on the lakeside was the fire station. On the other side was Lil John's restaurant and the old church.

The big event was on July 4th. The carnival came to town early. The very center was left empty, and then they would bring in railroad ties and start stacking them in a square. Each square inside the one below, going higher, until it was three stories high. Then they would bring an old car and, with a crane, lift it to the top. The fire department across the street would then light the bottom of the fire and all evening people would come to watch it burn down. I'm certain there were many wagers made on the exact time the car would fall. We just wanted to stay awake to see it.

Dick and I were living sort of separate lives. He continued to drink until he couldn't stand. The only time he would refrain from drinking was when he would be flying. He still had two licenses that I was certain of, for a Cessna and a Beechcraft. He co-owned the Cessna with a friend of his. Occasionally we would take it up for a ride. I had motion sickness, but this never bothered me. It seemed more like floating than moving. One day he said, "Let's go flying."

When we got to the airport we went to a different airplane. He said, "This is my friend's plane, a Star Duster II."

I said, "Ok."

It looked like a Snoopy plane to me. Turns out it was. He said, "You sit up front."

He pulled buckles up over each of my legs, then one over each shoulder, all to attach in the center to a master buckle. "This isn't dangerous, is it?"

"Oh no, it's quite safe. Besides, I'm the pilot."

A harrowing 20 minutes for sure. Seemed like an hour. Rollovers, flying upside down. I was terrified but lived to tell this tale. I would never take another ride.

3

Dick had now received his second DUI, and I was fully aware that he had a serious drinking problem. He denied it, of course. I spoke to his sister, Betty, the nurse. She didn't believe me: "I've never seen him drunk."

He was always fully functioning until he passed out. I was now sleeping fully dressed, believing that I would get a call from the police, the hospital, or the morgue. Late one night, I got a call from a police station in Maine, about 40 miles north of where we lived. They said they found Dick out cold in his car on the side of the road. They couldn't wake him, assumed he had been drunk but couldn't do a breathalyzer test. We'll keep him overnight. He showed up the next morning like nothing was unusual. I told him the police had called me. He said he was just tired and had missed the turn, so he'd pulled over to sleep. Really, it took him 40 miles to realize he'd missed the turn.

What I felt was the last straw was when I got a bill in the mail from Beneficial Finance asking for a payment on the $2,000 loan we had taken out last month. When Dick got home, I asked him what it was about. "I don't know."

"Did you get a loan from them?"

"I think I did."

"What did you do with the money?"

"I don't remember."

"You can't remember what you spent two grand on a month ago?"

"No."

I called Beneficial and said never send another bill with my name on it. I had no part in this. Had they called before, I would have told them not to give him the money because he'd never pay it back.

"But you're his wife."

True, but I didn't sign for the loan, he did.

Not much later was the big one; DUI number three. In Massachusetts, there's a three-strikes-and-you're-out law. It is mandatory that you lose your license for one year if you receive three DUIs while driving in Massachusetts. Maybe he'll learn now. Gulf Oil is very understanding; he's been a long-term employee. He is offered a transfer to dispatch for the year. It's a 10 p.m. to 6 a.m. shift. I now drive him to Boston, an hour's drive to his work, go to sleep, and get up at 4 a.m. to drive back to Boston to pick him up, take him home, then drive myself to work. About a month later I applied for a job at Anna Jaques Hospital in Newburyport, Massachusetts. Perfect, I'll work from 7 a.m. Saturday to 7 a.m. Sunday. Now I can drive Dick back and forth during the week and get some rest.

I love this job. They have a break room with a cot, but I don't sleep much. My job is X-ray tech, but this hospital is very busy. Two major roads, I-95 and 495. When nurses are busy, I help with triage, checking in patients. There is a small operating room in the emergency department. If someone comes in with a broken bone, I start taking an X-ray. Then, if necessary, I call the orthopedic surgeon and anesthesiologist on call. Then bring the patient into the OR. By the time the doctors arrived, I'd have scrubbed in, prepared the patient, and gotten the instruments ready. I help with the surgery and take X-rays after. Back to the ER, next patient, please.

I now have Dick's bills to pay and can't stand staying still. Dick now sleeps after I pick him up in the morning. So, I go over to a little restaurant on the Plains called the Plain Fare and get a job waitressing a couple mornings a week. Meeting townspeople and loving it. I joined the Powwow Pond Association and soon became a board member—I always have an opinion. Someone tells me they need a waitress up the street at the 1686 house. Of course, I apply—they need someone midweek. It's a very expensive restaurant so the tips are good.

Somehow Dick still manages to get a bottle of Jack Daniels to hide at home and walks to the store to get beer while I'm working. Why I thought he'd quit, I don't know, but I did.

The town had now begun a theater group. They were holding auditions for the musical *Anything Goes*. I couldn't resist. I tried out and got the part of Mimsy, the one with loose morals. A singing part. I met new friends:

Judy Oljey, who plays the lead; and the Diamonds—the mom, Pat, and her three daughters, Pam, Sarena, and Cheri. It was lots of fun. After rehearsals, many nights

Judy and I would go to Lil John's for a drink, where I met the owner, Marvin, and his barmaid, Joyce. Joyce also loved to sing and dance, so we would make it a party. Joyce asked if I would be interested in waitressing occasionally if they needed it. I said sure, I can always use another job.

Finally, Dick got his license back. But two weeks later he came home plastered. I told him to get out. He wouldn't go. He said, "It's my house."

I said, "When you move out, I'll come back. I'm not staying with you."

I went to Judy's, and after a few days Dick called and asked me to please come home.

I asked, "Why?"

He said, "There's laundry to be done."

"Anything else?"

He said, "The mail is piling up."

Again, I asked, "Anything else?"

He said, "Not that I can think of."

That was it! If he said even once, "Because I love you," I would have gone back. But he didn't, so I called a lawyer. I filed for divorce.

Within a week he had moved back to Haverhill with

a friend. I went back to the house. Indeed the mail was piled high and unopened. But the bathroom was unbelievable. The bathtub was filled with his dirty clothes. I called his sister, Betty, and told her I had filed for divorce. "You must be wrong; he can't really be a drunk." Blood is thicker than water.

I had an appointment with the lawyer. I told him Dick won't respond; he doesn't respond to anything. The lawyer says oh yes, he will.

Dick doesn't respond, of course. The lawyer says that because he didn't respond it's now a contested divorce, more money. I'm not even divorced yet and I've already been screwed by my own lawyer.

4

Anything Goes will be starting soon and we're all excited. Judy tells Marvin about my divorce, and he is sympathetic. Typical bartender listens to all the stories. I have planned a pool party at my house. I invite all the cast as well as Joyce and Marvin. Pat and the girls show up and the girls run and hug Marvin. "Hi Daddy!"

Marvin's last name is Diamond.

How did I not make the connection? They have the same last name. I hope I haven't been the cause of WWIII. Evidently it's okay, they have been apart for years.

With Dick gone I now take on another job at the Village Square Inn in Hampstead, New Hampshire, a family place with a bar side. I work in the dining room. Lots of regular patrons, good tips, and good food that I don't have to pay for. Still paying Dick's bills, mostly for guns, fishing equipment, and photography equipment. Silly I don't ever remember him taking any pictures. I was truly a fool. Even more so because in the divorce agreement I agreed to continue to pay all the current bills.

I just wanted to have him out of my life.

I really like Marvin; I consider him a friend now. Judy says, "You should go out with him."

"Oh no, that would ruin our friendship."

So, I held on still working my four jobs. Marvin eventually asked me out. He took me to a restaurant in Hampstead with wonderful German food, The Gasthaus Langer. We would go there often, and we became friends with the owners.

After one of our dates, Marvin asked: Could I please help you with your bills? Absolutely not! I knew if I were to ever have a chance with him, I could not feel as if I owed him anything.

I will work like a dog and pay all my bills myself. But thank you.

Divorce final, bills all caught up. I was finally free. We had a particularly cold night and Marvin called and asked if Leonard, who had now moved back from Arizona, or my brother Lenny could come fix a frozen pipe. I called Leonard and he said he couldn't go but the shop was open. Called Lennie and he said the same. So I stopped by the restaurant to look at the problem. I went to the shop and got my supplies. The frozen pipe was exposed over the sink in the kitchen. Marvin found a wide plank and placed it over the sink. I was standing on the plank with a blowtorch in my hand soldering the pipe. This could all be seen from the bar where a group of guys were now standing. "Marry that woman, Marvin!" They were chanting.

Christmas day was here. Marvin gave me a card that I still have. In it, he said, *If you would like, I will move in with you for one year, and if it works out, at the end of the year, we'll make it more permanent.* Of course, yes. That was perfect.

Eric makes a few visits; he will be marrying a nice Jewish girl. We talked about some good memories. Since Marvin is Jewish and my belief is now that my faith is a relationship between my God and myself, I have decided to convert to Judaism. I want the Rabbi to marry us.

I made an appointment with Rabbi Press. First, he

starts, we don't like to convert people. And why would you want to be a Jew? Even us Jews don't want to be Jews. I told him about Eric and Bible College. And I said it doesn't matter what you decide. I believe that I am already a Jew by virtue of having learned about Jesus and doing as he asked. In Bible school I learned what Jesus said not to do. Now most of these religions went back to doing all the things he abolished. I am a purist; my faith is between me and my God. I don't need a pastor, a pope, or a Rabbi.

He said, "Good, that's a start."

A few more weeks of meetings, mostly trying to dissuade me. I'd ask a question like, "What do Jewish people think about this or that?"

Always the same answer: "It's not about them, or us, it's about you. You have a question, you ask God. You'll know the answer for you. Like you said Nancy, it's a relationship between the two of you. You had the answer all along."

Having passed the classes, I was to participate in the Immersion Mikvah ritual. It took place at an orthodox temple where I was stripped of all my clothing and adornments. Wrapped in a towel. The Mikvah was vacant except for the attendant. She beckoned me into the pool of warm water. I recited my learned prayers and went totally under the water, staying under until I felt everything bad about me was gone. I did feel like a new woman.

5

The year was passing, and we were doing great. Marvin's friend Eddie called one morning and told Marvin he had to drive to Seattle to pick up his son's motorcycle. It'll be three days out and three days back. Want to come with me?

"I'll call back and let you know. Nancy, do you think you can handle the restaurant for a week so I can go with Eddie? Close the bar, count the money, make deposits, etc."

"Sure, I can handle that."

He called Eddie back. Ed said he'd be at the restaurant in 20 minutes. We went to meet him. Said our goodbyes and they were off. But the story of that seven-week Odyssey is for another book.

The next autumn we were talking about this permanent thing. We both wanted to eventually get away from the cold winters. And I said, "Here's the deal. If we get married, I won't cook. I hate to cook, I don't want to learn to cook. I'll do plumbing, set tile, lay hardwood floors, but I don't cook. You cook, got it?" Agreed—important things taken care of.

One day as we were driving through town, I said, "There's my uncle's house." I thought he was going to drive off the road. He said, "What uncle?"

"Uncle Al. Al's Rod and Gun Shop. He's my uncle."

Silence persisted. The next day we were at Vera's having tea and cookies, as was our tradition. Vera was Marvin's ex-mother-in-law and long-time bookkeeper. I told her about Uncle Al. She laughed. When Marvin was in the bathroom, she said, "So, Bridgette is your cousin?"

"Yes."

Then Vera told me that Marvin had been engaged to Bridgette a little while ago. I'd had no idea; I hadn't seen Bridgette since I was a really little girl.

Marvin and I finally talk about Bridgette. He says she thought we would marry, not me. She did come by the restaurant a bit later, to check me out I assume, but didn't venture to talk. I was told later that she was really hurt and had believed they would marry.

It was August and Marvin said, "We should put your place on the market. It should take months to sell, so now's a good time."

Marvin and his friend Dian are real estate agents. One business was never enough for Marvin. So, Dian lists my place and we set the price a little higher, so we have room to go down. We got a call right away. We have a full-price offer, and they want to close immediately. They want to put their kids in school here for September. What do I do now?

Marvin says, "Take it. I'll take care of the rest."

I went to work for the next weekend. He called the hospital and said, "You're all moved in here. The dogs are in the pen outside."

He and some of the boys from the bar had moved all of my things to the room above the back dining room. Closing was fast, and the check was deposited into my bank. A couple days later the bank says I have an overdraft. Impossible. I went straight to the bank with my deposit slip.

They said, "Ok, don't worry." They find the teller has keyed one digit wrong in the account number. "We'll fix it by Monday."

"Oh no," I said, "You'll fix it now."

"But it's Friday."

"I'll sit here and wait for a statement with my real account today. Whoever got that money could be in the Bahamas by Monday."

Reluctantly they gave me my statement. I was rich, I had never imagined that much money. Marvin said to put it into a Certificate of Deposit in my name.

"But it's our money now."

"No," he said. "That's your money. You worked hard for it. It will be for whatever you want it for."

Ok, a CD it would be. Incredibly the rate was at a whopping 16.5%. Now my head is reeling, I can't comprehend it.

The wedding is scheduled for December 6th. Service and reception in the brand-new function room at the 1686 House. By November 1st it looks like they're working on the renovation but it doesn't look promising. I stopped in to talk to the owner, Peter. He said not to worry. It will be open by Thanksgiving.

I was to call and make honeymoon reservations for a week at Kutsher's Country Club in the Catskills. They asked for a credit card number. I told them we don't have one.

They said, "How are you going to pay?"

"With cash."

"We can't make a reservation without a card."

So, I got my first credit card. I stopped by the 1686 House to find the room we reserved would not be ready for our wedding.

I tell Marvin.

"Alright, I guess I'm catering our wedding."

He makes the shopping list. I work on the setup for the service in the back dining room and call the guests to explain the new plan. Marvin spends the last day preparing. Prime rib and lobster tails. With a mountain of cream cheese and a ring of lox at the bottom. Rabbi Press is performing the service. He will be amused, not offended, by the lobster.

6

I stayed at my mother's new house, on the Massachusetts/New Hampshire border, the night before the wedding. I woke up that morning to a blanket of white. On December 6th we are having an unexpected blizzard. The street has over a foot of snow. I called Marvin, he said don't panic. They're already plowing the parking lot. The gas stove is ready for food. There's no power yet, but I have plenty of wood in the fireplace, so the place is nice and warm.

I don't remember what time the wedding was. I was just certain that I was not going to make it. But my mother had a friend who worked for the city. She called and 30 minutes later a plow was plowing the streets all the way to the main road. Thank you, Jimmy! I called and let Marvin know the road was clear. He said the food is cooking and the band is here and set up. No electricity yet but don't worry.

I was now dressed in my white dress. White, at the prompting of Vera, Pat's mother. "This is the real thing, and you have never had a wedding like this before, so you wear white."

Leonard let me off at the back door and parked around the corner on the street. The power was now on, Rabbi Press was here. The band was playing. Everything's ready. Leonard has my arm. Amy, Marvin's granddaughter from marriage number two, is a flower girl, happily throwing rose petals on the floor. No wedding march; the song "Turn Around," by Rod McKuen, was sung by Darlene. Darlene has been friends with Joyce since childhood and sings with her band. We walked to the chuppah where Arnie, Marvin's oldest child from marriage number one, stood as best man with his dad. Marvin was so handsome, so surreal. Arnie stepped down to where my mother, my maid of honor, stood. I walked up to meet Marvin. Just before the ceremony began, Marvin's best friend Eddie said from the front row, "It's not too late to change your mind, Marvin. The motor home is waiting out front."

The ceremony was beautiful. We had a single pair of

beautiful pink crystal wine glasses that I loved. One was wrapped in a napkin and would be stomped on by Marvin to symbolize the fragility of marriage.

We remember the destruction of the temple, but faith remains. As we believe our relationship will. And it has.

We danced to our song, "Camelot." Feasted and headed out on our honeymoon. We would spend our first night at a local hotel, then travel in the morning to New York. In all the excitement, we hadn't eaten much. We were hungry, so we went across the street to the Chinese restaurant. While we were enjoying our dinner, Eddie was trying to get access to our room to interrupt us. The clerk refused to give him our room number. So he went back home disappointed.

Kutsher's was beyond belief. Never had I been to a place where I was treated like a queen. Great entertainment every night. Food to die for, complete with a Jewish mamma to say "Eat more, you're too skinny. Have another dessert."

FINAL PUZZLE PIECE

Marvin is what I had spent all these years waiting for. No judgment. He loves me as I am. Calls me his aging hippie.

I thought my journey had ended but it was just beginning. From childhood abuse to self-deprecation and depression, and now to a princess with a man who truly loves me. Do I wish my life had been different? Sometimes. But I am truly happy with the woman I am. And if I could get through this puzzle of life, so can you!

Perhaps a new puzzle is in order!

What do you think?

If you have read my book and are dealing with abuse of any kind, be strong. Today the situation has improved. People will listen. The strong man is not always right. You have power!

It took me years to find mine; my wish is that you will find yours now!

I had no intention of writing a book. 70-plus years later, the man in now gone. So now I can remember and write. Then read what I'd written and begin to heal. By gone, I mean that the man is now deceased. As any survivor of abuse knows, if the abuser is still above ground, you are AFRAID. Even if they are miles away. A picture, something that someone says, these can all trigger a response you cannot control. This followed me until the end of his life.

So, I felt I needed to publish this book. As healing for me, and as a reassurance to those who now need hope. Nowadays, there are resources for you that were not there for me. I have realized I love to write and tell my stories, so there are at least two more books in the pipeline.

I am available at my email,
marnan96@hotmail.com, or
on my Facebook page, Nancy E Diamond.

Other Resources:
National Coalition Against Domestic Violence.
NCDVH.org. 800-799-7233.
Victimconnect.org. 800-273-8255.

ABOUT THE AUTHOR

Nancy was born and raised in Haverhill, Massachusetts. She graduated from Addison Gilbert Hospital School of X-Ray Technology in a Co-Op program with Northeastern University in Boston, Massachusetts. She spent 52 years in the medical field and is now a self-employed tax preparer with her husband, Marvin.

This is her first Book.

Facebook:
https://www.facebook.com/nancy.felker.diamond/

Made in the USA
Middletown, DE
19 April 2024